The power behind your need is in your seed!

7 Lessons for a Lifestyle of Giving

Dr. Amanda Goodson

™

No part of this publication may be reproduced or transmitted in any form or by any means, mechanical or electronic, including photocopying for recording, or by any information storage and retrieval system, without express written permission from the publisher.

ISBN-13: 978-0615748696

ISBN-10: 0615748694

Copyright © 2012 by Dr. Amanda Goodson - All Rights Reserved.

Unless otherwise indicated, the scripture quotations are taken from the Spirit Filled Bible, New King James Version. © Copyright 2002, Nelson. Used by permission of Nelson Publishing. All rights reserved.

Printed in the U.S.A.

Second Edition

The power behind your need is in your seed!

7 Lessons for a Lifestyle of Giving

Dr. Amanda Goodson

™

Spiritual Quick Books

Acknowledgements

I dedicate this book to my family, church, ministry team and ministry partners. For those who love to give, I give God glory for you!!

TABLE OF CONTENTS

Acknowledgements

Introduction   7

    1. About Your Need   13

    2. The Blessing of Tithing   19

    3. The Blessing of Giving   25

    4. The Blessing of the Seed   29

    5. Sowing and Reaping   33

    6. Time and Talent   39

    7. Excellence in Giving   43

    8. Giving as an Ambassador   49

Conclusion   54

Bible Verses About Giving   57

Bibliography   67

About the Author   69

Introduction

Anyone out there in need? Anyone out there with a giving heart? We all have needs and are expected to have a giving heart in order to activate the blessing and the favor of God. His Word promises to open up the windows of heaven to those who choose to believe Him and His Word. Also, there is an abundance of blessing granted to those who plant seed. In time, they will see a harvest.

Want to unlock your full potential and influence others around you in a more powerful way through your giving? Want to engage with your ministry team or community to achieve peak levels and activate the many blessings of God available to us? Want to be creative in your giving? This book is developed to answer these questions and more.

Kingdom-minded people have the power to make things happen that will transform their community and ministry in profound ways. Unlocking your giving potential is an essential part of reaping a harvest. This book contains several keys that will unlock your giving potential and develop a lifestyle of giving.

People who utilize the lessons highlighted in this book will see remarkable improvement in their giving and have their needs met in awesome ways. It is God who supplies and multiplies your seed. He disperses abroad and is no respecter of persons. What He does for one, He will do for others. Those who act on the Word of God will see results.

We believe that we all have been granted the ability to accomplish great things. Greatness has many facets and levels. Greatness carries power; and the power to carry out our tasks can be done well with the right desire.

Put an expectation on your seed, enhance your life through your seed, and see how God will tremendously bless your giving.

The information in this *Spiritual Quickbook™*, *"The power behind your need is in your seed,"* will serve to equip you with tools that will provide valuable insights into how to give and receive what you need according to God's purposed destiny for your life. You will also serve to transform the lives of others around you, your ministry and your community.

Givers that have a command of what the Word of God says walk in a dimension of authority that is remarkable. They understand the blessings of tithing, the blessing of giving seed, the blessing of time and talent, and the blessing of sowing and reaping a harvest.

This book is meant to arouse your thinking and cause you to be more creative, enhance your knowledge of the

Word, and develop a giving lifestyle that will impact others around you with power. As you read these pages, keep an open mind so that you will be able to see how unlocking your giving potential will affect you.

At the end of each chapter, we have provided space for your personal reflections and notes. Enjoy reading, and discover the power behind need is in your seed!!

About Your Need

"And my God shall supply all your need according to His riches in glory by Christ Jesus. Now to our God and Father be glory forever and ever. Amen."
(Philippians 4:19-20)

"Ask, and it will be given to you; seek, and you will find; knock, and it will be opened to you. For everyone who asks receives, and he who seeks finds, and to him who knocks it will be opened. Or what man is there among you who, if his son asks for bread, will give him a stone? Or if he asks for a fish, will he give him a serpent? If you then, being evil, know how to give good gifts to your children, how much more will your Father who is in heaven give good things to those who ask Him! (Matthew 7:7-11)

God is the Supplier of all that we need. We are either on the way to the blessing and favor of God, or we are in the middle of God's blessing.

Although it may seem tough, God is always there. Hannah needed (desired) to be blessed with a son, in the pit Jacob needed his promised blessing to show up according to his dreams, and the woman at the well needed to know about the living water. Needs/desires/dreams are not always financial; but no matter what the need, God will supply it.

There may be some individuals who have a need to feel connected. There may be some who have a need to know that they are making an outstanding contribution. While others need to gain insights in how to solve a pressing problem. Some need financial abundance and blessings, and others may simply need to know the Word better.

So that there is no confusion, there is a distinct difference between a "need" and a "desire". There are many things that we think we absolutely need. However, in God's eyes a true need is anything that is essential to fulfilling His purpose for us. A true need is a deficiency, or a lack or shortage of something essential in our lives.

On the other hand, a desire is not an essential, but rather it is something that is enjoyable in the process of fulfilling God's purposes. A desire is a yearning or a longing for something that we would like to have to enrich our lives.

Every individual possesses three (3) basic areas of need and desire:

1. The physical;
2. The psychological; and
3. The spiritual

Some of our physical needs and desires consist of food, clothing, convenience, a comfortable place to live, the pleasure of being touched by another human being, and healing from illnesses.

The psychological part of us includes the mind, the will, and the emotions. We long to feel loved, secure and significant in our human relationships. We long for companionship and intimacy with others, and we desire to see our loved ones come to know Christ.

Our spiritual needs are the most crucial of all our needs. Their fulfillment is absolutely essential in fulfilling God's purposes for us and in making us whole. We cannot live eternally with God unless this particular need is met in our lives. If the spiritual need is unfulfilled, then we will experience spiritual death; which is the loss of relationship with God in the earth realm and total separation from Him throughout eternity.

The Lord has promised to give us the desires of our heart; but the condition for receiving those desires is that we first delight ourselves in Him (see Psalm 37:4). Delighting ourselves in Him means that we become soft or pliable. The expansion and enlargement of that which God wants to bless us with has a direct correlation to our obedience and willingness to delight in Him. In Psalm 21:2, the king (David) stated that God had given him his heart's desire and had not withheld the request of the king's lips. Wow!!

One of the limitations that humans have is an inability to know which of our physical and psychological longings are essential to God's purposes. This is why we need to delight (open our mouth to God, be soft and pliable) in the Lord. When we desire more than anything else to have what God wants for us, then we can be sure that He will fill every desire because we are yielding totally to Him.

The key to claiming God's promises so that we do not continuously yearn for that which does not fit into God's purposes or wait endlessly for a "need" to be met that does not fit the definition of a true need in God's eyes, is simply this:

1. Our <u>need</u> should be to find the *truth* of being completely loved, unwaveringly secure, and unchangeably significant spiritually because of our relationship with Christ.
2. Our <u>desire</u> should be to *feel* loved, secure and significant physically and psychologically.

I believe nothing is too hard for God and He will honor our requests according to His purpose. Only God can determine which of our needs are important to fulfilling His purposes, and only He knows whether the fulfillment, or the lack of fulfillment, of our desires will assist in fulfilling His purposes.

God promises to provide for the needs of His children. He provides for their physical needs for food, clothing, and shelter. He provides for their spiritual needs through prayer, Bible study and ministries in His Name. He provides for their personal needs through intimate relationships with Himself and with other believers.

God will provide for His children as they seek His help through prayer. He desires to provide for our total well being; spiritually, physically, and even materially. His source of supply is limitless.

No matter what, God is the only Supplier that will meet all of our needs according to His riches by Christ. He gets the glory for meeting our needs, forever and ever.

Our needs are met according to what we believe about God. Our needs will continue to be met by allowing the Word of God to work for us and by us working the Word.

I want to encourage you to think about your future and your purposed destiny, and then shape your thoughts around God meeting those needs today and enabling you to reach that place. This includes healing, long life and deliverance.

By understanding this godly principle, we will never be in lack or need. Just ask, seek, knock…God will answer and supply your need.

Leader Reflections:

What do you need God to provide or do for you right now? How will this transform and shape your future? Make a list in the space below.

The Blessing of Tithing

"'Bring all the tithes into the storehouse, that there may be food in My house, and try Me now in this,' Says the LORD of hosts, 'If I will not open for you the windows of heaven and pour out for you such blessing that there will not be room enough to receive it. 'And I will rebuke the devourer for your sakes, so that he will not destroy the fruit of your ground, nor shall the vine fail to bear fruit for you in the field,' Says the LORD of hosts; 'And all nations will call you blessed, for you will be a delightful land,' says the LORD of hosts."
(Malachi 3:10-12)

There are some who have a misconception about the purpose of tithing. The purpose of the tithe is simply our way of acknowledging, trusting and showing God that He is our Source and our Creator, and that we have what we have because of the gifts, talents, and abilities that He has given to us.

The importance of tithing is seen as a two-fold act. First of all, tithing is an act of worship. We worship God through our tithes by acknowledging and reverencing that everything comes from the Lord, including all the skills, talents, and abilities we utilize to obtain work and earn a living.

Tithing spiritualizes our attitude toward money, and it makes our sacrifice of giving a way for us to declare what we value the most. As a direct result, God can then use our tithe to release us from the grip of the love of money, since the tithe has now become a sacred activity affirming that He is the Owner of all things.

Secondly, tithing is an act of faith. By tithing you are demonstrating your faith in God and His goodness. Upon doing this, you are now in a spiritual position to receive God's response, which is the promise to bless and give you much more.

When God says that He will open a window and pour out a blessing that there will not be room enough to receive, I believe that this means that our blessings will be so vast that they will appear like an avalanche of blessings to us here on earth. Further, I believe that when God opens up His windows to us, we can see, perceive and discern that every blessing that comes will be from Him, and Him alone. He will choose whatever avenue He pleases to get the blessing to us. We should be in position and have a posture to receive from our Heavenly Father.

Through our tithing, God has promised that the Host of the Armies in heaven will perform and secure your abundance of blessing. Tithing is a godly principle that will activate a specific outcome from heaven with a promise from God. No other person can make this promise – absolutely no one.

Tithes and offerings are a godly principle/law that reap benefits from heaven. Here is what the Lord of Hosts says:

- *"I will open for you the windows of heaven"*
    - We first saw the windows of heaven open up in Genesis 7:11 during the time of Noah when God poured down rain from the sky. Then later in Malachi's time, the people needed the windows of heaven to open upon their fields. Because of their sin, God had sent them a drought and their crops were dying.
    - Malachi encouraged them to stop making God's ministers live in poverty and to start bringing their tithes and offerings again. They were assured that by doing so, their needs would be provided for, plus there would also be a profit.
    - This principle still applies today. God blesses our efforts when we tithe.

- ***"Pour out for you <u>such</u> blessing"***
    - God desires to see His people blessed. However, before the people were given the blessing, they were issued a challenge and asked to put God to the test. The condition for the blessing was predicated on their obedience. They had been robbing God, and when this happens, God cannot bless disobedience.
    - God wants to prove Himself; He wants to show Himself strong in the lives of those who will trust Him (those who have faith in Him) and who obey Him.
    - When these two attributes are working together, God's Word is true and can be trusted. He always keeps His promises.
    - The word "such" is HUGE!
- ***"There will not be room enough to receive it"***
    - Our complete and absolute faith, trust, and obedience in God assures us of the blessing. The ***"faithful man will abound with blessings,"*** (Proverbs 28:20) and ***"the generous soul will be made rich. He who waters will also be watered himself."*** (Proverbs 11:25)
    - The principle here is that generosity in your offerings, by God's blessing, secures the increase; while stinginess actually leads to poverty instead of expected gain.
- ***"I will rebuke the devourer for your sakes so that he will not destroy the fruit of your ground"***
    - The term 'ground' in this text refers to soil, agriculture, fruit and produce. Ground

represents increase or production. As is known, the ground (soil) increases or produces a harvest upon the seed that is sown within it.
- o God has promised to watch over the ground (the productivity) of the tither. The devourer cannot destroy, nor does he have access to, that which God has protected and shielded.
- *"the vine will not fail to bear fruit for you in the field"*
  - o This indicates that everything that the tither produces will not only be protected, but everything the tither does will come to harvest.
  - o The harvest signifies the finished product or the increase. ***"But he who received seed on the good ground is he who hears the word and understands it, who indeed bears fruit and produces: some a hundredfold, some sixty, some thirty."*** According to Matthew 13:23, the minimum increase is thirty-fold.
  - o The tither can fully expect that everything that he or she sets out to do or accomplish will be completed and that the increase will be great.
- *"All nations will call you blessed, for you will be a delightful land"*
  - o The faithful tither is compared to land or soil. But this time the reference is to a delightsome land or a land filled with delight.
  - o God intended for tithers to live in delightful productivity and have pleasure in their business pursuits – and that others would be able to see it and recognize it.

God does keep His promises. He truly opens the windows of heaven and pours out His blessings upon those who are faithful and who obey His commandments. However, His blessings are done in His own way. They may come in a financial way, or they may be realized by a spiritual outpouring. His blessings may even come in unusual ways that we may not readily recognize; but the promises of the Lord are certain and absolutely guaranteed.

Leader Reflections:

In the space below, list 2 or 3 additional thoughts about transforming your life right now and receiving the blessing of God through your tithes and offerings. How can you apply this godly principle and expect great things from God?

The Blessing of Giving

> *"Give, and it will be given to you: good measure, pressed down, shaken together, and running over will be put into your bosom. For with the same measure that you use, it will be measured back to you."*
>
> *(Luke 6:38)*

This is another promise from God. When you give, it is God actually providing back to you as a form of blessing for your faithfulness to Him. He sees our giving as us giving to His people – which is like paying it forward.

As a mother, it pleases me to see others give to my family and others in need. It automatically puts me in a state of wanting something great to happen for the giver.

Since God's principle of giving is such a powerful principle, I believe it will catapult us to a dimension and realm of unbelievable power.

This realm is one where you divide your blessings with others and God will give back to you, without measure.

Luke calls it:

- Good measure
- Pressed down
- Shaken together
- Running over

We are instructed to first seek the Kingdom of God in order for all the promises to be received. The Kingdom is inside of each of us. The only thing lacking is our knowledge of how to apply these laws/principles in order to operate within our Kingdom mandate. In our state of ignorance, we fail to benefit from this great gift. The Kingdom actually includes an abundance of all things from the Lord that are good.

When giving, the important thing to remember is to stop operating in the kingdom of man and begin to operate in the Kingdom of God. In other words, we have to change that which is governing us by transforming our thinking. For example, within the kingdom of man a bushel of wheat can make enough of bread to feed several people.

However, when that same wheat is planted in properly prepared soil, it enters the Kingdom of God where it can be multiplied and eventually feed a multitude; like taking two fish and five loaves of bread, feeding a multitude, and still having twelve baskets of bread remaining after all have been fed (see Matthew 14:13-21; Mark 6:31-43; Luke 9:10-17 and John 6:5-15).

The idea of putting a seed into the ground and getting thousands of seeds in return may seem strange. However, if you knew for a fact that what you have given, or sown, would multiply the same way that seeds multiply when properly planted, then everyone would want to become givers of seed. What we lack is the knowledge of how to apply the laws and operate within that Kingdom. In our state of seeking God differently we can grow to benefit from that which Christ has given us.

Some may have trouble believing, but it only takes one bountiful harvest/miracle to change your life. For example, we don't have to understand the laws of electricity to turn on a light switch and receive light, nor understand the law of the harvest in order to make a seed grow when it is properly sown. The law of electricity that lights our homes and runs our computers has always existed, but it was not harnessed until recent generations. Similarly, by using the laws of internal combustion and aerodynamics, we can lift an aircraft weighing tons off the ground and travel farther in an hour than our ancestors could travel in a year.

Our faith in these laws is established by seeing the end result. In order to harness these laws and enjoy the blessings that come from them, we have to begin applying the principles. If you put a seed into the ground and care for it correctly, then you can expect it to germinate, grow and return to you multiplied. But if you scatter seed on top of the ground, the birds will eat most of it, the wind will blow some away, and the remaining seed will most likely become scorched by the sun and eventually die.

Consider the seeds that you have sown. Were they planted in good soil, properly cultivated and harvested? Or were they scattered and somehow lost or burned away?

Leader Reflections:

In the space below, list additional thoughts about the blessing of giving that inspires you to give to others and how this characteristic enhances your relationship with God. In what areas can you make improvements?

The Blessing of the Seed

"While the earth remains, seedtime and harvest, and cold and heat, and summer and winter, and day and night shall not cease." (Genesis 8:22)

"For the land which you go to possess is not like the land of Egypt from which you have come, where you sowed your seed and watered it by foot, as a vegetable garden; but the land which you cross over to possess is a land of hills and valleys, which drinks water from the rain of heaven, a land for which the LORD your God cares; the eyes of the LORD your God are always on it, from the beginning of the year to the very end of the year." (Deuteronomy 11:10-12)

Everything that emanates from us can be considered a seed. The words we speak are seeds. Our ability to influence others is a seed, our choices are seeds, our thoughts are seeds, and the way we spend our time is a seed. I am constantly reminded of this fact by my one of my spiritual leaders and friend, Dr. Laura Thompson.

The question we need to ask ourselves is, how does seed germinate? How does it sprout, take root and grow? We already know that if the elements are there – the soil, the water, the temperature, light, etc., then the seed reacts to its environment and germinates. What is not known is why this all takes place.

It happens because, through His Word, God has set a law in motion of seedtime and harvest. Galatians 6:7 teaches, **"Do not be deceived, God is not mocked; for whatever a man sows, that he will also reap."** The blessing of the seed occurs when putting the law of seedtime and harvest to work for you.

The blessing of the seed is in giving – giving of your time; giving of your talents; and giving of yourself. To gain friends, one must give themselves over to being friendly. If you want loyalty from others, it starts with you being loyal. If you expect forgiveness, then you first must be able to forgive. If you are in need of a financial blessing, then the prescription is to sow a financial seed.

God will always supply you with seeds, even if they are very small seeds to start out with. Keep sowing, and then watch the seed grow like the mustard seed into a very large harvest. The law of the harvest works. However, we must be careful and remember that Jesus is Lord of the harvest, and He must remain as the only thing that we truly rely on.

This law works not only in life situations, but in terms of money also. Whatever a man sows, that he will also reap.

Leader Reflections:

List 3 to 5 notable seeds that you planted over the last month. Also, identify 5 areas where you can plant more seed. What harvest are you expecting right now?

Put additional notes and reflections on this page:

Sowing and Reaping

"Then Isaac sowed in that land, and reaped in the same year a hundredfold; and the LORD blessed him."
(Genesis 26:12)

"But this I say: He who sows sparingly will also reap sparingly, and he who sows bountifully will also reap bountifully. So let each one give as he purposes in his heart, not grudgingly or of necessity; for God loves a cheerful giver. And God is able to make all grace abound toward you, that you, always having all sufficiency in all things, may have an abundance for every good work. As it is written: 'He has dispersed abroad, He has given to the poor; His righteousness endures forever.' Now may He who supplies seed to the sower, and bread for food, supply and multiply the seed you have sown and increase the fruits of your righteousness, while you are enriched in everything for

all liberality, which causes thanksgiving through us to God." (2 Corinthians 9:6-14)

The principle here is clearly self-evident – the harvest is directly proportionate to the amount of seed sown. When a generous believer obediently gives by faith and trust in God, then God gives a return on the amount that was invested. Invest a little; receive a little; and vice versa. Luke 6:38 reminds us, ***"…For with the same measure you use, it will be measured back to you."***

We are also not to give ***"grudgingly or of necessity; for God loves a cheerful giver."*** Remember, the tithe is an act of worship. To worship God grudgingly, or with an attitude of regret or out of an act of duty or obligation, implies that you are in some manner being coerced to do it. God freely gives His love to us, and He desires for us to do the same in return.

God has a unique and special love for those who are happily committed to generous giving. He loves a heart that is delightfully excited about the pleasure of giving. Moreover, He also gives seed to the sower. He supplies you with seeds, even if it is a very small seed to begin with. Someone once said, 'if what you have in your hand is not enough to meet your need, then that is your seed.' In other words, keep sowing and then watch it grow like the mustard seed into a great harvest.

Remember, Jesus is the Lord of the harvest, and He will increase your service as you seek His Kingdom. He gives liberally to us according to His Word, and you are fully assured of having everything you need to be successful in doing what God has planned for your destiny.

We are blessed to be a blessing to others. It is part of the principle of sowing and reaping. My husband grew up on a farm, and when his family wanted to reap a crop they would always plant a seed. If they wanted corn, they would plant corn seed. If they wanted beans, they would plant bean seeds. If they wanted watermelon…well, you get the picture.

In leadership, one must apply the same principle. If you want to lead with authority and unlock the power of your full potential, you must be willing to invest the time into becoming the leader that you expect to become. You cannot sit around waiting for things to happen. You must go out and make things happen around you. I know you might need to work on an area to make a great contribution, but if you do not start today, it will be a long time coming.

To unlock your full potential in giving and be a person of influence for the kingdom of God in your workplace, school, home, or community, you must first believe from within that you can accomplish it. I believe you have the ability to do anything you put your mind to do (through Christ, of course). I believe there are laws that govern us when we seek to do things the wrong way. The end result is that our wrong efforts will eventually cause us to end up going nowhere or get off track.

I am not talking about doing wrong. I am talking about doing the right thing; planting the right type of seeds of greatness and receiving back more than you invested.

Consider the farm analogy again; to get a crop or harvest of corn, my husband's family would plant a certain amount of seed and would reap a great harvest from that seed. I believe that as you seek to unlock your potential, solutions to your most pressing needs will become available to you as you seek them out (as you plant seeds).

Try it! You will be amazed at the results. I know it works...I tried it and stand very successful in life. I do not want to take my blessings for granted. I continue to plant seeds by coaching and leading and inspiring others to be greater. I am very grateful for the opportunity–it works!! Now, go plant a seed of greatness and reap an outstanding harvest!

Leader Reflections:

In the space below:

1. Make a list of the things you can start doing right away to reap a harvest (make your seed work for you according to the word of God).

2. What can you do better in your job/church/community to be a leader of influence?

3. What will you teach others about what you have learned by your example?

Put additional notes and reflections on this page:

Time and Talent

"Blessed is the man who fears the LORD, Who delights greatly in His commandments. His descendants will be mighty on earth; The generation of the upright will be blessed. Wealth and riches will be in his house, And his righteousness endures forever. Unto the upright there arises light in the darkness; He is gracious, and full of compassion, and righteous. A good man deals graciously and lends; He will guide his affairs with discretion. Surely he will never be shaken; The righteous will be in everlasting remembrance."

(Psalm 112:1-6)

When we think about the gifts that we utilize in terms of time and talent, we are really talking about the practice of stewardship, and returning a portion of our gifts to God – not because He needs them, but because we feel an overwhelming need to demonstrate our love and gratitude to God. When we give of ourselves through our time and talent, we establish an example of discipleship; which is one of the primary requirements for building the Kingdom, as set forth by the Great Commission.

This is also another way of describing the life of a disciple. It really means that you are willing to recognize and receive your God-given gifts with a grateful heart, you agree to cherish and develop them in a mature and responsible way, and you agree to share them in justice and love in celebration of God's glory. Further, you also agree to return them with increase to the Lord.

Time is a precious commodity. Everyone is given gifts of time, talent and treasure. The question is how are you utilizing those gifts. All of us are given the same amount of time daily, weekly, monthly and yearly. I believe time can be redeemed. God exists outside of time, but He created time for us so that we would have a system within which to function.

Some think they do not have enough time to do their daily tasks. Some think they do not have enough time to read, worship, pray or serve.

I would like to share with you that time is a seed. Wherever you sow it that is where you will reap a harvest. The same thing applies to your God-given abilities and talents. They are both given by God and should be used to give God glory. I would rather spend my time investing in my God-given purpose than being idle.

Time is a gift and should be treated as something valuable to God. Your talents and abilities come directly from the Father. You are able to do exactly what Jesus did and greater. You have the ability to move mountains, speak to your destiny, call forth your progress and reap the benefits.

The problem that many face is the difficulty in teaching and in the practice of stewardship. What is needed is a clear understanding of exactly what stewardship is and being able to embrace it.

Stewardship is:

- Dependence on God. Recognizing that all of our gifts and talents come from Him, and that we take credit for nothing.

- Gratitude. Living a life of gratitude and taking the time each day to recognize the gifts that God has given to us and being grateful for them.

- Giving back. Returning a portion of our gifts back to God with gratitude and love.

- A love response. When we allow God to truly abide in our hearts, we will automatically feel the need to join our lives with Him and dedicate our time and talents to carrying out His work.

- Proportionate giving. Realizing that we are all called to give as God has given to us. We can no longer base our seed on what others are giving, but we give in direct proportion to all God has given to us.

- Accountability. Realizing and recognizing that we will be expected to give an account of all that we have done with our God-given gifts.

- Thankfulness. Thanking God daily and also being willing to show gratitude, recognition and appreciation for the gifts that others have given.

- <u>Trusting in God</u>. Believing that God will always provide for us.
- <u>Discipleship</u>. Striving to put God first in ***all*** things and to follow wherever He leads us.

Leader Reflections:

Consider what types of gifts of time and talent you possess; and in your moments of reflection, which images emerge for your life, and in which directions are the decisions of your life leading you? Make a list of 3 to 5 things that energize you and which endeavors in your life have been especially fruitful.

Excellence in Giving

"'If anyone has ears to hear, let him hear.' Then He said to them, "Take heed what you hear. With the same measure you use, it will be measured to you; and to you who hear, more will be given. For whoever has, to him more will be given; but whoever does not have, even what he has will be taken away from him."
(Mark 4:23-25)

To continuously unlock one's giving potential one must consistently walk in the excellence of giving. This requirement for excellence is exemplified through our immediate uninhibited and unreserved obedience, such as the behavior that can be seen in a small child. This is the type of obedience that does not question or debate God's motives, or demand to have an explanation or a list of other options to weigh prior to making a decision to give.

An example of this type of excellence in giving can be seen in a good friend of mine; I'll call her KC. KC has always been very determined to succeed and goal-oriented, as well as being extremely talented and creative in many areas; but she wasn't raised in church and grew up in a household that was unsaved and somewhat dysfunctional. In spite of this, she was always drawn to the church and had a desire to attend church and serve in ministry.

KC faced many challenges and had to overcome many obstacles when first coming to and determining to serve the Lord, but she believed every Word that God spoke; especially when it came to the principles of giving. She aligned herself with strong godly mentors, and quickly resolved to do exactly as the Word of God instructed – never fail to tithe from the first fruits of her earnings, and **always** include an offering. She also took every opportunity to sow seeds into the ministry; hers as well as others in the community, as God directed.

The result of KC's creativity and determination, coupled with her dedication and excellence in giving, quickly resulted in many doors opening to her. Although quite young (under the age of thirty), she is currently a very successful businesswoman and entrepreneur, and a high recognized and respected leader in ministry on many levels.

KC discovered the key to unlocking her potential – consistency and excellence in giving. She never did it with the goal of becoming rich and famous. However, understanding the principles of giving, she prayed to God for His direction and blessing, listened for His voice, received His vision for her destiny and purpose, set a goal for her ministry and her business, and then set forth to do all that He required while proceeding in His timing and in His will.

The individual who can successfully unlock his/her full potential is able to hit the target, on target. They understand the power of being purposed and assigned to do a task. They never do it alone; unless assigned to do so. They seek strong and wise counsel, and they encourage others to excel in an outstanding manner. No matter the task, they seek ways to improve and excel in extraordinary ways. Excellence does not stop until the task is done well and the solution is effective.

1. Have the ability to dream–reframe your thinking about giving to realize your full God-given potential. Set an example of excellence for others.

2. Know your vision and mission for giving – it is strategic.

3. Develop a plan for giving and saving, and then work toward that plan.

4. Use your giving to meet the needs of others. It will transform the lives of those around you.

5. Use your ability to give with the right attitude using the gifts given by God.

6. Know how to leverage your best seed to get things done around you. Let your seed work for you.

7. Strive for excellence in your giving, thought life, influence, decision, authority, will and gifts.

8. Be persistent; do what others are not willing to do, or cannot do.

9. Be willing to stand for what you believe and value in your giving.

Just as our physical muscles require regular exercise to become strengthened and powerful, the same applies to the exercise of giving. As you faithfully trust God and exercise the principles of giving, your faith will increase in direct proportion to the blessings you will reap resulting from your giving and sowing.

An avalanche of blessings is inevitable when you follow cyclical godly principles of giving; be ready for it. You will be in awe of God – He does not lie.

Leader Reflections:

In the space below:

1. List additional thoughts about being excellent in your giving?
2. What are your expectations for the future?
3. In what areas are you a increasing in your giving and receiving a harvest? (List 3-5)
4. If Jesus were to ask what resources you needed to be more excellent for Him, what would be on your list?

Put additional notes and reflections on this page:

Giving as an Ambassador

"I will make you a great nation; I will bless you and make your name great; and you shall be a blessing. I will bless those who bless you, and I will curse him who curses you; and in you all the families of the earth shall be blessed." (Genesis 12:2-3)

"Now then, we are ambassadors for Christ, as though God were pleading through us: we implore you on Christ's behalf, be reconciled to God. For He made Him who knew no sin to be sin for us, that we might become the righteousness of God in Him." (2 Corinthians 5:20-21)

People who unlock their godly authority in giving should recognize that they are also powerful ambassadors. An ambassador is typically an individual who has been sent as a high official, a delegate, a messenger, or an emissary to a particular place with an assignment from the government or organization that they support. As I have written in other books, the ambassador is vital to the success of an organization or government. Sometimes, ambassadors are assigned to be an instrument of peace, and other times they carry an important message abroad to other governments. In some cultures, only those who would be willing to give careful consideration to the risk of their lives and invest all would be considered worthy of such an assignment.

A true ambassador is one who will be willing to represent their government, country, or organization with their best efforts in order to carry out the assigned mission or message in an outstanding way in their giving. This isn't just the act of giving up all their material wealth and possessions, but total and absolute unconditional surrender of self to complete their assignment. Giving as an ambassador will affect nations and God will give you more to accomplish your designated assignments.

An ambassador's commitment to give of his/her vast resources has to be without any reservations. In order to be a true ambassador of power, a person must be willing to give, lead or advocate for an assigned cause for the government or organization that they represent in a way that gets results.

An ambassador's authority is far reaching. This assignment and authority requires an abundance of resources to bless the nations.

Your giving will have an assigned expectation (verbally expressed by you) to go into areas that are considered to be hard to reach and get the Word, food, cloths and water areas to be an influence for their government or organization. Other times, the assignment may seem easy. In either case, the ambassador understands that he or she has been charged with an assignment to complete and successfully influence the territory around them by giving. With this understanding, proper training, clear vision, and goals of the organization, the ambassador is fully equipped as they are going through their delegated assignment; they have the assurance of an outstanding successful harvest.

Those who are willing to become ambassadors of giving will discover that one of the vital requirements is the willingness to forsake all for the Kingdom. In other words, you must have a changed mindset and no longer choose to live according to the kingdom of man, but you must make a prayerful, purposeful, deliberate and conscious choice to live according to Kingdom of God.

The kingdom of man believes in satisfying one's personal needs and giving to oneself first; and if there is anything left over, then giving a token offering to God. The Kingdom of God requires giving to God from your first fruits, and includes a seed offering as well. Choosing to live according to the Kingdom of God means you are not willing to continue clinging to or safeguarding any secret self-indulgences in order to satisfy the desires of the flesh.

The ambassador for the Kingdom of God must be one willing to carefully assess the cost of the assignment and invest all that God has provided to him or her. This requirement is more than divesting oneself of material possessions. It is an absolute, unconditional surrender of your way of thinking and developing a willingness to live in accordance to that which the Lord commands in the Word.

In reaching your giving potential, see yourself as an ambassador of power on an important assignment or task for your organization and influence using the ambassador mindset. Take your assignment seriously, transform the way you think about the assignment, and focus on being an outstanding seed sower.

Remember; give responsibly with the mindset of an ambassador and unlock your giving potential.

Leader Reflections:

In the space below, list the assignment you have that will put you in a position to serve and give your church, community or civic organization with integrity as a powerful ambassador?

Conclusion

We trust that by implementing the keys in this book, you will begin to see remarkable improvement in your relationship with God and in your giving at all levels.

As stated in the introduction, Kingdom-minded people have the power to make things happen that will transform their community and ministry in profound ways. Unlocking your giving potential is an essential part of reaping a harvest. This book contains several keys that will unlock your giving potential and develop a lifestyle of giving.

People who utilize the lessons highlighted in this book will see remarkable improvement in their giving and have their needs met in awesome ways. It is God who supplies and multiplies your seed. He disperses abroad and is no respecter of persons. What He does for one, He will do for others. Those who act on the Word of God will see results.

We believe we all have been granted the ability to accomplish great things. Greatness has many facets and levels. Greatness carries power; and the power to carry out our tasks can be done well with the right desire.

Put an expectation on your seed, enhance your life through your seed, and see how God will tremendously bless your giving.

The information in this mini book, *"The power behind your need is in your seed,"* has served to equip you with tools that will provide valuable insights into how to give and receive what you need according to God's purposed destiny for your life. You will also serve to transform lives of others around you, your ministry and community.

Givers that have a command of what the Word of God says walk in a dimension of authority that is remarkable. They understand the blessings of tithing, the blessing of giving seed, the blessing of time and talent, and the blessing of sowing and reaping a harvest.

This book is meant to arouse your thinking and cause you to be more creative, enhance your knowledge of the Word, and develop a giving lifestyle that will impact others around you with power. Through these pages, I trust you kept an open mind so that you will be able to see how unlocking your giving potential will affect your future.

At the end of each chapter, I trust you filled out the sections in the provided space for your personal reflections and notes. At the end of the conclusion, I have provided you with bible verses about giving that you should prayerfully study, read aloud dand meditate on daily.

Thank you for reading our book, and enjoy your journey as you continue to unlock your giving potential and live an awesome life!!

I look forward to seeing you in the next *Spiritual Quickbook*™!

Bible Verses About Giving:

Please prayerfully and carefully study these verses and adopt them daily as you continue on your giving journey. Seek to read 2 or more of them aloud daily. At the end of this section, please document additional scripture about giving that you discover during your personal study time.

Deuteronomy 10:17-18

[17] For the LORD your God is God of gods and Lord of lords, the great God, mighty and awesome, who shows no partiality and accepts no bribes. [18] He defends the cause of the fatherless and the widow, and loves the alien, giving him food and clothing.

Proverbs 22:9

[9] A generous man will himself be blessed, for he shares his food with the poor.

Proverbs 29:7

[7] The righteous care about justice for the poor, but the wicked have no such concern.

Matthew 6:3-4

[3] But when you give to the needy, do not let your left hand know what your right hand is doing, [4] so that your giving may be in secret. Then your Father, who sees what is done in secret, will reward you.

Matthew 6:19-21

^{19}"Do not store up for yourselves treasures on earth, where moth and rust destroy, and where thieves break in and steal. ^{20}But store up for yourselves treasures in heaven, where moth and rust do not destroy, and where thieves do not break in and steal. ^{21}For where your treasure is, there your heart will be also.

Luke 6:35

^{35}But love your enemies, do good to them, and lend to them without expecting to get anything back. Then your reward will be great, and you will be sons of the Most High, because he is kind to the ungrateful and wicked.

Luke 6:38

^{38}Give, and it will be given to you. A good measure, pressed down, shaken together and running over, will be poured into your lap. For with the measure you use, it will be measured to you."

John 3:16

^{16}"For God so loved the world that he gave his one and only Son, that whoever believes in him shall not perish but have eternal life.

Acts 10:22

[22] He and all his family were devout and God-fearing; he gave generously to those in need and prayed to God regularly.

Acts 20:35

[35] In everything I did, I showed you that by this kind of hard work we must help the weak, remembering the words the Lord Jesus himself said: 'It is more blessed to give than to receive.'

Romans 8:32

[32] He who did not spare his own Son, but gave him up for us all—how will he not also, along with him, graciously give us all things?

Romans 12:1

[1] Therefore, I urge you, brothers, in view of God's mercy, to offer your bodies as living sacrifices, holy and pleasing to God—this is your spiritual act of worship.

Romans 12:13

[13] Share with God's people who are in need. Practice hospitality.

2 Corinthians 8:2-5

²*Out of the most severe trial, their overflowing joy and their extreme poverty welled up in rich generosity. ³For I testify that they gave as much as they were able, and even beyond their ability. Entirely on their own, ⁴they urgently pleaded with us for the privilege of sharing in this service to the saints. ⁵And they did not do as we expected, but they gave themselves first to the Lord and then to us in keeping with God's will.*

2 Corinthians 9:11

¹¹*You will be made rich in every way so that you can be generous on every occasion, and through us your generosity will result in thanksgiving to God.*

Ephesians 4:28

²⁸*He who has been stealing must steal no longer, but must work, doing something useful with his own hands, that he may have something to share with those in need.*

Philippians 4:19

¹⁹*And my God will meet all your needs according to his glorious riches in Christ Jesus.*

1 Timothy 6:18

¹⁸*Command them to do good, to be rich in good deeds, and to be generous and willing to share.*

Hebrews 13:16

^{16}And do not forget to do good and to share with others, for with such sacrifices God is pleased.

1 John 3: 17-18

^{17}If anyone has material possessions and sees his brother in need but has no pity on him, how can the love of God be in him? ^{18}Dear children, let us not love with words or tongue but with actions and in truth.

Deuteronomy 15:10

^{10}Give generously to him and do so without a grudging heart; then because of this the Lord your God will bless you in all your work and in everything you put your hand to.

Deuteronomy 16:17

^{17}Every man shall give as he is able, according to the blessing of the LORD your God which He has given you.

1 Chronicles 29:9

^{9}Then the people rejoiced because they had offered so willingly, for they made their offering to the Lord with a whole heart, and King David also rejoiced greatly.

Proverbs 3:27

^{27}Do not withhold good from those to whom it is due, when it is in your power to do it.

Proverbs 11:24-25

^{24}There is one who scatters, and yet increases all the more, and there is one who withholds what is justly due, and yet it results only in want. ^{25}The generous man will be prosperous, and he who waters will himself be watered.

Proverbs 21:26b

^{9}...the righteous gives and does not hold back.

Proverbs 22:9

^{9}He who is generous will be blessed, for he gives some of his food to the poor.

Proverbs 28:27

He who gives to the poor will never want, but he who shuts his eyes will have many curses.

Malachi 3:10

^{10} "Bring the whole tithe into the storehouse, so that there may be food in My house, and test Me now in this," says the Lord of hosts, "if I will not open for you the windows of heaven and pour out for you a blessing until it overflows.

Mark 12:41-44

^{41}And He sat down opposite the treasury, and began observing how the people were putting money into the treasury; and many rich people were putting in large sums. ^{42} A poor widow came and put in two small copper coins, which amount to a cent. ^{43}Calling His disciples to Him, He said to them, "Truly I say to you, this poor widow put in more than all the contributors to the treasury; ^{44}for they all put in out of their surplus, but she, out of her poverty, put in all she owned, all she had to live on."

Luke 3:11

^{11}And he would answer and say to them, "The man who has two tunics is to share with him who has none; and he who has food is to do likewise."

Luke 6:30

^{30}Give to everyone who asks of you, and whoever takes away what is yours, do not demand it back.

Luke 6:38

^{38}Give, and it will be given to you. They will pour into your lap a good measure, pressed down, shaken together, and running over. For by your standard of measure it will be measured to you in return.

Acts 20:35

^{35}*In everything I showed you that by working hard in this manner you must help the weak and remember the words of the Lord Jesus, that He Himself said, 'It is more blessed to give than to receive.*

Romans 12:8

^{8}*Or he who exhorts, in his exhortation; he who gives, with liberality; he who leads, with diligence; he who shows mercy, with cheerfulness.*

2 Corinthians 9:6-8

^{6}*Now this I say, he who sows sparingly will also reap sparingly, and he who sows bountifully will also reap bountifully. ^{7}Each one must do just as he has purposed in his heart, not grudgingly or under compulsion, for God loves a cheerful giver. ^{8}And God is able to make all grace abound to you, so that always having all sufficiency in everything, you may have an abundance for every good deed.*

2 Corinthians 9:10

^{9}*Now He who supplies seed to the sower and bread for food will supply and multiply your seed for sowing and increase the harvest of your righteousness;*

Philippians 4:15-17

[15] *And you yourselves also know, Philippians, that at the first preaching of the gospel, after I departed from Macedonia, no church shared with me in the matter of giving and receiving but you alone;* [16] *for even in Thessalonica you send a gift more than once for my needs.* [17] *Not that I seek the gift itself, but I seek for the profit which increases to your account.*

James 2:15-16

[15] *If a brother or sister is without clothing and in need of daily food,* [16] *and one of you says to them, "Go in peace, be warmed and be filled," and yet you do not give them what is necessary for their body, what use is that?*

Put additional scripture and notes here:

BIBLIOGRAPHY

Dr. Amanda Goodson. *Authority of a Leader.* Tucson, AZ, 2012.

Dr. Amanda Goodson. *Powerful People Lead.* Tucson, AZ, 2012.

Frederick Cross, Dr. Amanda Goodson, Odetta Scott. *How to Unlock Your Full Potential*, Tucson, AZ 2012

Antony Robbins. *The Power to Shape your Destiny: Seven Strategies for Massive Results.* CD, 2012.

Antony Robbins. *Unleash the Power Within: Personal Coaching form Anthony Robbins.* CD, 2012.

New American Standard Bible, Updated Edition, 1995.

Exhaustive Concordance of the Bible. (Lahabra, CA: The Lockman Foundation -- Foundation Publications, Inc. Anaheim, CA); 1981, 1998.

The Spirit Filled Bible (NKJV). (Nelson Publishing), 2002.

Merriam-Webster's Collegiate Dictionary. (Merriam-Webster); 10th Edition, 1998.

Munroe, Dr. Myles (1954-), president and founder of Bahamas Faith Ministries International.

www.BibleGateway.com

http://www.inspirational-bible-verses.com/giving-bible-verses.htmlBusinessdictionary.com.

http://christianpf.com/21-bible-verses-about-giving/
http://www.openbible.info/topics/gift_giving

About the Author:

Dr. Amanda H. Goodson

Goodson is a native of Decatur, Alabama and currently resides in Tucson, Arizona where God has entrusted her to serve as Pastor of Trinity Temple Christian Methodist Episcopal Church. She also plans and facilitates seminars, workshops, and retreats for the CME church.

She is President and on the Board of Directors for Never the Same Ministries (NTS), a God-inspired, Tucson based, Kingdom ministry dedicated to serve as a vessel through which people are provided tools and resources to develop a more spiritually mature and improved relationship with God through Christ. The NTS God ordered mission is to provide biblically based instruction, tools, and coaching for people within the community through planning and deployment of conferences and events across the United States.

God has gifted Goodson to be a Spirit-led preacher, teacher, trainer and coach for churches, agencies and non-profit organizations. Goodson connects with her audiences by sharing the Word of God through real-life experiences. She gives God glory as He allows her to inspire others to learn more about being a Spirit-led Christian in the world today. God has blessed her with an enthusiastic, energized and interactive method.

Goodson is fully committed to the Lord and knows that she has a blessed Spirit-led life. Her purpose is to fill the earth with the knowledge of God's glory by serving the Lord boldly through her ministry; bringing others closer to Christ and introducing Christ to those who have not accepted Him as their personal Savior. God's Word is her authority. Goodson believes that God's presence and power is Almighty and worthy to be praised. Further, she knows that God will make great things happen through His people.

Amanda has a Bachelors of Science in Electrical Engineering from Tuskegee University, a Masters of Science in Management from Florida Institute of Technology, and a Doctor of Ministry from United Theological Seminary specializing in church administration.

She is married to a godly man and has one a son.

As a Kingdom citizen, she is fully submitted to the will of God. Her prayer is to be active in sharing her faith, to make her thoughts agreeable to the will of God, and to have the mind of Christ. The Word of God is the final authority in her life.

For a complete listing of CDs, DVDs, and books by Dr. Amanda Goodson, or to participate in a ministry conference, book a conference, speaking event or training, please email or visit the following web site:

NTSMinistries@aol.com
or visit
amandagoodson.com

Books by Dr. Amanda Goodson

Spiritual Quickbooks™
Kingdom Character
Spiritual Authority
Carmel Voices
The Power to Make an Impact
Powerful People Follow Christ
Step out in Faith
Going Higher, Declarations for Kids
On the Rise
Thoughts from God
Spiritual Intelligence

Leadership Minibooks™
The Authority of a Leader
Character of a Leader
Unlock Your Full Potential
12 Power Principles for Administrative Professionals

Photo by Martha Lochert

www.ingramcontent.com/pod-product-compliance
Lightning Source LLC
Chambersburg PA
CBHW032214040426
42449CB00005B/584